for the

CRACKS

and

POTHOLES

in our lives

August Irons

ISBN   979-8-218-24320-3

Sky Island Signature   Wolcott, Vermont

I thought I must let her go.

I knew she wouldn't object.

But what was really needed

was to let self go.

That would have changed

the way she saw me.

In the garden there is a familiar sound;
it is the buzz of busy bees and beetles,
where abundant food fills their cupboards.

In the garden there are familiar scents;
of chamomile and sage, marigold
and lavender.... and that of moist earth.

In the garden there are many colors;
reds and yellows and endless other
among the dancing shades of green.

In the garden there is quietude,
a song in the heart, and the memories of Mom,
who taught me the way of the garden.

I looked her in the eye and said, "You're walking around as if asleep, girl, and it's on a slippery slope; it's slippery and treacherous and you don't appear to realize it. It gets worse farther down. If you don't stop this, will you make it out alive and ok? Probably not."

She looked down as she shuffled her feet in the snow, then suddenly looked up and into my eyes – something she had never done. "You don't know how that makes me feel, hearing that. It makes me feel even less confident. I don't know how to get off this dangerous slope you think I'm on. Maybe you could not say anything, maybe you could just take my hand and gently lead me back to something solid and not leave me here alone. You're all I have, Grandpa. You're the only one who understands."

I don't think she realized that she had just breathed new life into my purpose to go on living.

Admission

I cannot tell you that I contributed to her gaining greater confidence in herself, or in making changes that make life easier. But I can say that our tumultuous relationship has uncovered difficult-to-accept traits that we share, traits that she cannot hide as seamlessly as I have nearly my whole life. Turns out I was a fool. I have denied a sense of inadequacy, knowing but explaining away my lying and distrust. I denied my self-absorption. I was always more lost than I was able to acknowledge. I had doubts about the wisdom of having a relationship with her when our paths intersected, thinking that her disabilities and insecurities were sure to make her a high maintenance gal. I did not need another charitable project in my life. But today I think our relationship was the best medicine I didn't think I needed. I am glad that I am so imperfect that I was allowed to penetrate her world and was *unable* to defend mine .... and that she could tear down my façade. Now I am free, committed to look for the learning in every shared thought, story, poem, and prayer.

Barefoot Kelly

Memories flood me of the day we met,

my mind's tethered and in strain,

back and forth like a fish in a net,

knowing I may never see her again.

She broke through an aged crust,

came barefoot on across and

touched me in innocence and trust,

and whispered, "I'll never forget you."

Ah, but she is young and travels on wanderlust,

roping the highway and things she adores,

youthful and caught up in dreams of lust,

groveling under broad-leaf canopies on a forest floor,

while here in the silent hills I go on

tending my goats and in pastures kind,

praying for her return in morning's dawn,

and for now finding ease in this dark wine.

Years have passed but the memories remain,

like stumbling upon bones in nearby fields,

my sanity is lost in the wine's bane,

still hoping for her at each new dawn.

High in the mountains the sun shines,

the winds howl and gusts sting,

setting the lines in men's faces.

The holly shivers.

An aging man, bronzed and hair wild,

determined to be as undauntable,

stands leaning into the mighty wind.

The wind gives.

Billowing gun-metal clouds

roll across the ridges like tanks,

and soon hail pounds the unprotected.

A volley breaks boughs.

The old man must give as did the wind,

and finds a degree of refuge

beneath an aged and fallen pine;

It had failed to give.

It is over more quickly than it had arisen,

as if but testing for willingness to give.

The sting remained yet the man offered thanks.

For the fallen tree.

The wind is free to be brutal,

caring not of right or wrong,

and woodlands and grasses weep.

The sun returns.

The wind has fallen.

The weathered man continues his run,

just as his father did,

and his father's father.

The wind will return, and gusts sting,

clouds will bring darkness

and black silhuettes a chill.

Vigor will give.

A man may find he lies safe

beneath a shelter of the broken,

and there is nothing more to do

but lie and listen.

There is always a voice after the storm.

It is a whisper,

a tincture in time.

The holly shivers.

I remember the morning that a friend, a Lakota-Sioux man, stood outside my open cabin door, looking upon the eastern sky. I heard him say as if to himself, "What a beautiful day to die."

A few minutes later, he was romping with the dog, playing 'Who gets the tennis ball?'

That changed my life, for I knew he meant it.

The Pair

I was seeing them in the early spring.

But then one day they were gone.

Now mid-October I look out my kitchen window

and there they are again.

They seem to know each other so well,

as if they know what each the other

is thinking or sensing or fixing to do.....

this pair of red-breast robins

of which I am envious.

Connection

Connection

Two years ago I wrote about a pair
of robins whom I envied
for their moving connectedness.
I think I was so taken with them
because they as well appeared
to enjoy watching me through
my kitchen window.
It is also that I am convinced
they've been lovers
for a long time.

It is now early June of another year,
and only one has returned,
spends most of her time
standing on the dirt road out front,
turning to the east,
then south, then west.....
watching, waiting.

Occasionally I would see her
just outside the kitchen window
where they used to hang out,
and on occasion I'd see her fly up

to a high limb of the old sugar-maple
on the far side of the road,
but not once did I see her
feed - not once.

For five days she waited.
Yesterday she was gone.
Tonight I will light a candle.
I know how it feels,
left behind and
not knowing why.

She's Back!

Hanging out by the window,
watching me move about,
and she looks great.

Into the kitchen and
first to the window
I too stand there long.....

I suspect this robin and
I have been wanting,
holding a wish,

that this new window
remains open, that it does
not slowly slide down.

So beautiful is she, even if lonely,
as she floats down from a high branch
to touch lightly upon solid ground.

Almost

Almost allows "at least you tried"
but also leaves a gap.
Almost makes an agreement
a broken agreement,
Almost makes a promise a lie,
can get you fired,
and harm a marriage.

Yes, I called for justice.

I revealed my own arrogance in thinking
that I know enough, that I see through
enough, to judge then condemn. That is
me choosing a blind eye to underlying
lies, a denial of pleasure in vengeance.

It is folly to talk of evolving
while continuing to deny
what we are. Bottom line is,
inflicting 'justice' does not heal.
Love may.

Finding the Lost While Lost

He met her

while looking to sell his guitar.

She was clearly

much younger

and seemingly not wanting

to be noticed.

They conversed

lightly, nervously,

and when he touched her arm

she moved closer,

speaking softly.

It was odd, he thought;

she is not that pretty,

yet I am transfixed.

A youthful face

of, say, sixteen.

He gave her the guitar.

She asked to see him again.

He stumbled for what to say,

it would be wrong, he thought.

It's the age difference, he said.

She touched his arm,

"I'm thirty", she said,

"You thought I was sixteen, right?

I'm guessing you're in your sixties.

Age doesn't really matter, does it?

But I understand."

Upon that she turned and left.

Days dragged, tethered

to weighty questions.

Why would it be wrong?

How can one's heart and gut

be so amiss?

Some weeks later

a bird-song filled day

riding gentle breezes,

a note in the mail

from her,

will you come to dinner

please?

Her story was

like her hair,

a bit chopped,

and hypnotic.

It poured thickly

over his heart

a sticky darkness,

and he asked

for a second glass of wine.

She, of an unplanned pregnancy,

a stoney and starved soil

sprouting complications,

was by cesarean so premature,

yet then but days later

the necessary excision

of half her bowel,

necrotic from infection,

was another last ditch effort

to save a tiny girl

who refused to die,

condemning her to

needle sticks and cut-downs,

rotating voices,

beeping machines,

ever-changing hands,

and tethered to tubes.

She bore visible

genetic anomalies,

and as she grew,

learning disorders

joined the list of curses.

Awkward encounters

and unexplaned dismissals

became daily fare.

Her young tender heart

knew failure in everything;

she was different

and not good enough

and not understood,

not even by her parents

who argued she was but stubborn.

So she grew tough,

became invisible,

purposedly deviant,

lonely.

Even on birthdays

she walked alone,

soaking in music and reading

to drown out the echo

of those rotating voices

and beeping machines

that meant waiting for the next poke,

the next prick.

She thanked him

for joining her for dinner.

As he walked her home

she spoke of her love for music.

When they reached her door

he knew not what to say,

knew only that standing before him,

fragile and hesitant,

was one he hoped

was going to be

a part of his life.

As if she read him

she took his hand,

invited him to stay.

They talked long

into the night,

she resting in his arms,

purring and snuggled

as if she had never

known a thing so wonderful.

In the morning they shared coffee

by her single window

bathed in the early light

dawning a new day,

she resting her head

upon his shoulder.

She spoke of being warriors

sworn to peace, a potential

lying not in gift

but in commitment.

Months passed into years.

Though she smiled a lot,

he could see how she struggled

every day.

It broke his heart

every day.

We want to believe,

even if practical,

in magic,

and love,

and happily nestling

into the sunset.

But Life has its way.

So immense their differences,

so overwhelming her inborn challenges,

so intense their convictions,

so fierce their fights,

scars intractable,

they could not define

that something

that smoldered underneath,

so easily bursting

into flaming daggers.

Shared sunsets and

walks hand-in-hand

down their country road

were seldom pain-free.

Confused and weakened,

they cried together,

worried their love

would fall apart.

And so the day came when

she packed and left.

He stumbled numbly

across the pastures,

his raspy aging voice

breaking into screeches.

He wailed against

all gods and persons

who over her young years

wrought their evil

right down to her

tender innocent heart.

Time crawled and

he wished to die.

It was again then on

a bird-song filled day

riding gentle breezes,

a note in the mail

from her,

will you come to dinner

please?

Again they talked long

into the night,

she resting in his arms,

purring and snuggled

as if she had never

known a thing so wonderful.

He fought tears; she was

so pale and fragile,

yet it was she

comforted him,

smiling and reminding him

that they were indeed

warriors as mighty

as they were weak,

and as blessed

as they were challenged.

They had each other.

It's You

the first to come to mind upon waking,

the one missing from my treasured morning
coffee,

who the dog sits by the door waiting for,

who no longer is asking me all those
unnecessary questions just for talk,

it's you, in case you're wondering,

who's no longer baking bread filling the air and
my tummy,

nor waltzing toward me sideways, asking for a
hug and making me smile,

that has me going to the window every time I
hear a car slowing down,

and that I blame when I've forgotten to stop for
lunch,

it's you, in case you question if you're
remembered,

that is missing when the chocolate bar is shaved
and spread upon Breyer's Chocolate Truffle,

is absent when I lift my glass of wine to make a
toast,

responsible for the layer of dust on the
mooncar

and the slump the birds are in,

........and the dog,

and yes, for the drunken state of your
"Captain".

It's You.

THANKSGIVING

I am filled with gratitude

for the bounty on my plate,

and thinking of you as I eat,

friend who opened my eyes

to tiny wonders

and open skies.

I give thanks.

The last time I slept out on the ground and saw a night sky so filled with stars that I could read by their light was nearly 50 years ago in central Australia.

I've slept out a hundred times since then.

I go back-and-forth on whether to stay abreast of world news. I wonder how we can assuage the pain and despair. Some days I feel guilty about spending my time in a garden, or taking in the beauty that still exists in fields and hills, how flowers sway together in the breeze. I remember how in my twenties I walked a narrow dirt road that led to my favorite coffee bar and there watched locals sharing and looking out for each other.

It's nearly too bright to stare out

upon the new fresh snow,

and it's cold, the temp at 5,

yet woodlands beckon,

and so I pull on my boots.

The dog runs ahead on our usual trail,

while I pause upon the mossy bog

hidden by surrounding sheltering conifers,

then follow her into the woodlands

into a world of magic.

In a ray of sun I lift my face,

feel its warmth upon my cheek,

while every tree stands in silence

waiting for days to grow longer,

.... while eyes everywhere are watching,
curious.

Oh, if I could see them each and all

peering out the doorway of their burrow,

waiting out the winters harboring,

the raven perched above, holding silent,

my dog sitting patiently.

It is then I see you,

standing beside the tree you always choose,

smiling and more beautiful

than when I last saw you,

..... that was so long ago.

You, making my heart race,

in this woodland of magic,

this is why, day after day,

this same trail, Skye running ahead,

.... it's you.   It's you.

The Well of Forgiveness

lies in the eyes of my dog,

a glimmer in the depths,

a still water reflecting sky,

free to all, no encumbrance.

Her name is Skye,

an utterly devoted canine

who forgets the injurious,

offering in return

eyes of devotion

and a wagging tail -

saying it's ok,

rub my head if you still love me.

Can I do the same,

full forgiveness

without requisite deal,

simple and final?

My granddad says it takes a dog

a lifetime to help a man unlearn

what was pressed upon him.

I think no man is greater

than any creature

leaving the mark of their paw

upon the ground

of our existence.

Rainbow

A beautiful rainbow,
high and reigning
over the eastern range
brought me to kneel by Skye
and point, and she looked at me,
wagging her tail then following my gaze,
and she continued looking there.
I thought either she is still looking for
what it is I am staring at,
or dogs are not color-blind and she sees
that rainbow,
and it reminds her of you.

In the distance three peaks stand majestic and stark

against the birthing of light reaching out into

the deepest blue.

The change is imperceptible over a moment,

yet slowly transforms

the world.

I think of us, the beauty in what we do,

this dance despite wounds,

birthing light and opening our eyes,

sharing coffee and watching our children chasing
butterflies

in fields of flowers.

Walking Slippery Ice

Sometimes there's no other option.

Others walked about with impunity,

which made her angry, as she shuffled inch
by inch.

Nobody fell except she herself,

twice, hurting her wrist and knee.

I told her that being scared of falling

was the cause, not being on ice….

which made her angry as well.

I said I am sorry, what's wrong with me,

and that is when she took my hand.

That was twenty years ago.

She still takes my hand today,

walking slippery ice.

Together Heave

Comrades, we're bickering, fighting amongst each other, and in case you haven't noticed, we're lost at sea in a heavy fog, going in circles while a furious storm looms.

Come together now and cast overboard the needs we don't need. Our strength is in our hearts, not in our beliefs, for they are but what they are – beliefs. And the gold we carry, it likewise becomes dead weight, and they together will sink us rather than save us.

We are at core comrades. men with heart. It is time to gather on the deck, stand side by side and put our hands upon the oars, and with our heads beside our hearts together turn this ship around, head this baby toward shore once more, and there we will again turn our hands to the plow and wave to our neighbor regardless of creed; we will no longer pillage for gold, then fight between us.

Our children will thank us, and will follow our example and bless us for the healing, and they too will be comrades with heart.

Outside my window a towering fir reaches as if to pierce the perennial pregnant cloud-cover. On this occasion I wished it to open the heavens for light, even whispered a prayer to that end. For I had become a man who in recent times sees naught but darkness.

I turned to my dog. She searched my face, as she routinely does, and I always wonder what she sees. I glanced into the dark screen of my computer and there, my reflection. I looked quickly away. I felt like some evil had overtaken me, and recent thoughts now had me scared.

I returned my gaze upon the fir..... and there, above, a hole allowing light. I whispered "Cool!", and in the next moment knew myself shaken.

I'm doing fine now. But I still wonder.

It's a heartbreak

watching a fake

fearful of love

make the mistake

thinking she's not good enough.

She cries alone,

lives by the phone,

easily forgets a face,

and buries the bone

before it's seen light.

Bypassing tho wanting,

fearing and feigning,

let down so often,

a self slowly fading

in the abyss of unfaithfulness.

It's a heartbreak,

a once timid heart

now bruised and hardened,

lying in a dark place,

having never been loved.

a fresh snow fall today,

evergreens all covered in white,

and now a clear sky holding a full moon ....

not too cold....

all in stillness....

so beautiful,

little eyes watching from their cozy burrow,

thankful for the mystery of it....

such an example, the night....

being still.

Guidance

Years back I managed a small herd of goats. The young buck was a big boy, and most kept their distance even though he was friendly and gentle.

There were times while working that I'd get between him and his girls, and as they'd nuzzle against me, the buck wouldn't have it; he'd push his way in and challenge me.

And I would not have that, convinced that he had to know I was alpha. I'd wrestle him to the ground.

He seemed not to hold it against me...... and that somehow always irked me.

This did not change over the years, until one day during such a fray, I tripped, fell, my head hitting a rail. He could have nailed me good. Instead, he merely backed up and waited. I struggled to stand, and that was when Lovely, queen of the herd, came over to nuzzle me affectionately, then nuzzled the buck. The buck just stood there, gazing toward the distant mountains.

I, hurting and humbled, walked away.

He continues to challenge me when I step between him and his girls, but something has changed. I merely stand, eyeing him, then he steps forward and rubs against me. I gently run a hand along his spine.

He was born to defend, to assure, yet he is gentle.

Today, I stand beside him, for neither is greater.

When you say these things, I find myself bewildered. I am sorry; that's all I know to say. Reading things as you have and feeling as you say, I understand why you must leave all this. I cannot say I'll ever do better, I did not know I was so dense and blind. I hope things go much better for you out there. I will never forget you; you have been the sunshine in my life.

Resiliency stands upon Hope.

Love leans upon Hope, and Hope leans on Love.

The two sisters are known to create miracles.

SALVATION THROUGH EVIL

It came most insidiously,

stumbling through the hell

of loving a simple evil,

naked and irresistible;

an unabashed lover

who did not love me

but wished she knew how.

Now in my elder years

I know not much at all,

yet do see this innocent evil

lies in us all, in all creatures

of all walks and regions,

in meadows and woodlands,

synagogues and bars,

be they you or me,

eagle or mosquito,

predator or victim.

It is the harsh route

a salvation is realized,

and only in hindsight,

in the wake of ash and rubble,

stripped of facade,

bared to the bone,

that my vision is freed.

In her false innocence

a desperate game of love and conquer;

it had to be played out,

for me, for her.

You and I,

must know, and be,

the lost and the found,

the taker and the giver,

predator and protector,

both evil and good.

It is the blessed road

to knowing we know little,

and need not conquer.

Saved at last!

Pockets

A friend loved to stick her hand

Into one of my pockets and rest it there.

It wasn't to see what was in my pocket;

she enjoyed having her hand

feeling warm and tucked in.

Raised in the north country,

I grew up accustomed

to a minimum of 4 pockets

on me at all times;

I could not do without them.

Mark Twain knew well their import,

pebbles for the slingshot,

money found or "borrowed",

acorns just because they're cool,

nightcrawlers .... anything, really.

That friend is now my wife.

I make sure I'm wearing pockets that are easy.

I conceal a find and feign a look of guilt,

and she smiles and slips a hand in…..

and gives me a kiss.

The Womb

I entered the kitchen,

leaned on the counter,

noted chaff flying in the field.

I opened the window,

and a chilly breeze reached in,

ran its cold fingers

through thinning hair,

and down my neck,

causing me to shiver.

I closed the window.

I turned back to my work,

noted a sudden stillness,

went back to the window.

No flying chaff, no leaves dancing.

The birds had quit singing,

the dogs were cowering,

chiseled heads pointing

to a sky quickly growing dark

as if a blanket was being pulled

over the world.

Then as sudden the fierce WIND,

wild upon his mighty steed,

galloping in and about lawn and pastures,

executing tailspins and whirlwinds....

whipping grit through the open window -

into my face.

I slammed the window, swearing.

I knew why I trembled; It felt not

of mere coincidence, the grit.

It felt personal.

But a forenight I had dreamed

of the Sun-warrior Olk who envied

the strength of brother WIND,

and now suddenly he appeared,

piercing the darkening clouds

with a laser of light, then thundered

off upon WIND's billowy white steed.

Olk knew WIND would never forgive;

he would seek vengeance – forever,

and that would wear his strength thin.

The sky grew still darker,

and WIND's fury exploded.

It was awful, branches swaying,

leaves whirled until the young

were torn from their mother.

Still it grew worse, young trees literally

pulled from the earth,

and from the stronger trees

the screams of maidens who

had borne their first blossoms

that spring.

"Not fair!" I screamed,

"returning when I am but a mere mortal!"

Instantly the house swayed,

screeched in agony,

Its timbers flying,

then thrown to the ground,

my home in mere minutes

a discarded carcass.

I ran for the old oak

in the lower pasture,

a magnificent tree,

a totem of prayer,

unaffected by the barbaric.

She was, as always, a refuge,

even when the hell of the hardened

invaded fields and woodlands.

But WIND had stored his anger long,

and it had fermented,

and I feared that he could raze

the earth to annihilate all.

For moments then all was still,

and I knew all too well

that the worst was to come.

And so it was, In the upper field

a black vortex grew to enormity,

pulling the darkness into itself,

emitting a roar of a thousand lions.

Downward toward the lower pasture

he raced toward that oak

where I stood.

I ran hard and threw myself

Into the near gully,

watched him slam into her,

pull her root-and-all from the earth,

watched him strip her,

rape her, leaving her strewn about.

Twisting, dancing, his roar

turning to hideous laughter,

a tightened funnel so strong

he was turning soil like a plow,

and now turned toward me.

I ran for the little cave in the gully

where I had in younger years

learned to hide when I had to cry.

Hands over my ears, eyes closed,

I crouched within its sweet dampness.

It was somewhere in time then,

crouched within that womb,

my head between my knees,

knowing that was all I could do,

that the roar gave

to the soft crying of a woman,

the ole oak.

I crawled stiffly then,

from the sweet damp womb,

lifted my head and opened my eyes,

eyes that had not seen for too long

the thousand stars in the darkness.

I slowly rose, shaking and in awe.

It is odd somehow, we brothers

with the burden of maleness,

trying for the hearts of women

whose blossoms we were;

we seem never to learn.

Might will never win her heart,

carnage will only make her cry.

The WIND still lives,

I still spread the seed of oaks,

earth holds us tenderly,

and her warm and moist womb

is still the home....

I will return to.

Forever isn't Free, but it Lasts

When you entered my life, along with you came
sunshine and heartbreak.

I was sincere, hanging out under clouds and
circling in fog.

You would lean left and I would lean right.

Then you more left and me more right.

I couldn't see my lifetime of lies...

and you couldn't admit a policy of denial.

But you remained sunny and resilient,

and I was sincere and committed.

We are best friends now, no matter that we

sometimes capsize the canoe and get chilled to
the bone.

Some days are shitty and others are funny,

but we always find each other…. confident in
knowing,

forever isn't free, but it lasts.

On Morning Pond

I sit lazy in the slender belly

of my red canoe,

watching skittering mayflies

skirt dim shaddows.

A sun inches skyward,

promising warm breezes,

and the mayflles dance,

for the wings of the mayfly

must dry quickly else they succumb

in the shallows where

invisible fin and lithe arc of tail

steer hunger-driven trout.

I lay back against the center thwart,

waiting for the sun to bring warmth.

I am wondering if in the shoals

the unseen and covert

will try to take her away.

The Charge

The day after winter's solstice

sun warriors begin their march,

endure bitter days,

men shouldering bags of seeds,

while women guard swelling wombs,

hoping all will witness again

spring's new blanket of life.

Blessed be the men who carry,

cursed be those who take for granted,

the annual gift of renewed light,

seed for new life.

I watch you with him,

kicking up your heels,

dancing and twirling,

pulling him to you.

He's just your friend,

you reassure.

I'm trying to recall the

last time your pirouette

was for me, the

last time you pulled

me to you and whispered

with fire in your eyes.

But that's ok.

The Morning After

Did you hear the doves this morning?

Did you see them, perched on that barren
limb of the dying pine out back?

I think they were watching us as we sipped
coffee by our morning window.

I wonder if they were watching us last night.

Morning

Why would a heart, in pain for a loved one who
cannot love, sing praise?

For the wind through the trees and a raven on
the wing,

and the loon carrying her young upon her back

in the cove of Wolcott Pond this morning.

Why would one in repugnance for a man held
captive by self, choose to turn empathic?

Because we are gifted with a haze   to soften
the stark,

and a gentle hand upon the shoulder says "it's
ok,"

and that makes forgiveness so much easier.

For I have known a criminal who repeatedly
violates without thought,

who one morning without thought dove into
the waters to save one drowning.

And I have known the sun to lighten the way for the waking soul in longing,

then expose her unfaithfulness by noon.

It is not, I think, about being fair or right; for I would ask "fair to whom?"

But it does seem the morning brings truth and pardon,

as she does light and mist.

Life's Way

Gradually the thunder faded, the rain eased into a light drizzle, and the golden glow on the western horizon began to fade into a common dusk. I let my out-raised arms fall to my side, and slowly kneeled upon one knee, my eyes upon the heavens. I raised my glass, made a toast to you, and whispered coarsely a prayer that some miracle will spare our parting. But death is not avoidable. I am sorry, so sorry, that I've grown old on you.

Received a package, a box of goodies,

and at the bottom, something I never knew existed:

a photo of Mom and me on a day I'll never forget,

and a diary.

She believed in me in a way unfathomable to me.

I do not know what lies ahead.

Requirements, restrictions, boundaries.

Mom struggled with these and the consequences,

yet in humility and prayer became light.

The ground I stand upon feeds me.

The winds breathe in me their life.

Water bathes me, and Mom's prayers keep me from drowning.

If you were here

I'd have a fire going in the wood stove,
water on for tea,
toast in the warmer.
I'd put on my new sweater,
reign in my big ridiculous smile,
and offer to make breakfast.

Skye would be wagging her tail the
whole time.

Between

She leads me down to the lowliest places,

and I admit it is a descent that is
bittersweet.

I have felt grounded there, even delighted.

Life and Love soar the heavens one day,

lie making merry on a forest floor the next.

Yet on a line between are those who
became snagged as if hung out to dry.

I like to think I can soar today and grovel
tomorrow

and not get hung up midway.

Yet then I find myself lying indolent in pain

when after harbor lights, wine and kisses,
something stupid is uttered,

and then she's gone, our smiles sunken in
the bay.

So easily I am snagged on the line between.

My Beautiful

I am sorry, what I did, you feeling

vulnerable and me not noticing.

I could have given a simple nod

and smiled, a hand on your shoulder.

Instead, in one fell swoop

I left you floundering,

me too blinded to see that.

I am sorry, my Love.

I go home now, and you must go on.

My confidence in you is strong and sure.

Forgive those mired in self,

tend your garden and pull the weeds,

nourish those young and

challenged as you are,

and I promise, you will know abundance,

you will know your beauty.

Fulfillment will bless your humble days

until your sun sets, to allow

darkness its time as well.

Trust your efforts, fear not ridicule,

but most of all fear not Love.

What I leave is yours,

to help ease in some small way

your burdens, my Beautiful.